UNDERSTANDING DIVINE ARRANGEMENT

And we know that all things work together for good to them that love God, to them who are the called according to his purpose.
Romans 8:28 *KJV*

by

Franklin N. Abazie

Understanding Divine Arrangement
COPYRIGHT@ 2017 BY Franklin N Abazie
ISBN: 978-1-94513303-9

All right reserved. This book or any portion thereof may not be reproduced or used in any manner whatsoever without the express written permission of the publisher, except for the use of brief quotations in a book review. All Bible quotes are from King James Version and others as noted.

Published by: F N ABAZIE PUBLISHING HOUSE- aka, Empowerment Bookstore.

That I may publish with the voice of thanksgiving and tell of all thy wondrous works.
Psalms 26:7

To order additional copies, wholesales
or booking:
Call the Church office (973-372-7518),
or Empowerment Bookstore Hotline (973-393-8518)

Worship address:
343 Sanford Avenue Newark New Jersey 07106
Administrative Head Office address:
33 Schley Street Newark New Jersey 07112
Email:pastorfranknto@yahoo.com
Website www.fnabaziehealingministries.org
Publishing House: www.fnabaziepublishinghouse.org

This book is a production of F N Abazie Publishing House. A publication Arms of Miracle of God Ministries 2017.
First Edition

CONTENTS

THE MANDATE OF THE COMMISSION iv

ARMS OF THE COMMISSION v

INTRODUCTION vi

CHAPTER 1
1 What is Divine Arrangement 1

CHAPTER 2
2 Partnership With The Holy Ghost 22

CHAPTER 3
3 Covenant Connection 33

CHAPTER 4
4 Prayer of Salvation 75

CHAPTER 5
5 About The Author 87

THE MANDATE OF THE COMMISSION

"The moment is due to impact your world through the revival of the healing & miracle ministry of Jesus Christ of Nazareth.

I am sending you to restore health unto thee and I will heal thee of thy wounds. Said the Lord of Host."

ARMS OF THE COMMISSION

1) F N Abazie Ministries-Miracle of God Ministries (Miracle Chapel Intl)

2) F N Abazie TV Ministries: Global Television Ministry Outreach.

3) F N Abazie Radio Ministries: Radio Broadcasting Outreach.

4) F N Abazie Publishing House: Book Publication.

5) F N Abazie Bible School: also called Word of Healing Bible School (W.O.H.B.S)

6) F N Abazie Evangelistic Ass: Miracle of God Ministries: Global Crusade

7) Empowerment Bookstore: Book distribution.

8) F N Abazie Helping Hands: Meeting the help of the needy world wide

9) F N Abazie Disaster Recovery Mission: Global Disaster Recovery.

10) F N Abazie Prison Ministry: Prison Ministry for all convicts "Second chance"

Some of our ministry arms are waiting the appointed time to commence.

INTRODUCTION

"And we know that all things work together for good to them that love God, to them who are the called according to his purpose."
Romans 8:28

Simply defined, divine arrangement is the hand of God in the life of a man/woman. We cannot comprehend the ways of God in the energy of the flesh. Often God uses the foolish things of this world to conform the wise. Often times God never do anything for us the way we expected Him to do it. It is written *"For my thoughts are not your thoughts, neither are your ways my ways, saith the Lord. For as the heavens are higher than the earth, so are my ways higher than your ways, and my thoughts than your thoughts."* (Isaiah 55:8-9)

"Before I formed thee in the belly I knew thee; and before thou camest forth out of the womb I sanctified thee, and I ordained thee a prophet unto the nations."
Jer 1:5

Although the above scripture strongly revealed the reason God formed us, and made us in His image. The preceding scripture below reveals God's divine plan and will over our lives. Divine arrangement therefore means recognizing the plan and pattern of God for our lives.

> *"For I know the thoughts that I think toward you, saith the Lord, thoughts of peace, and not of evil, to give you an expected end."*
> **Jer 29:11**

> *"Now when they had gone throughout Phrygia and the region of Galatia, and were forbidden of the Holy Ghost to preach the word in Asia, After they were come to Mysia, they assayed to go into Bithynia: but the Spirit suffered them not."*
>
> **Acts 16:6-7**

We must therefore develop a relationship and fellowship with the person of the Holy Spirit, for unless we depend on the Holy Spirit on every issue of our lives, we will end up in frustration.

> *"Moreover whom he did predestinate, them he also called: and whom he called, them he also justified: and whom he justified, them he also glorified."*
> **Romans 8:30**

In my own theology nothing happens casually. Every event is invented by God through the person of the Holy Spirit. It is written: *"For God is not the author of confusion, but of peace, as in all churches of the saints."* (1 Cor 14:33)

We must therefore respect, honor, and acknowledge the leading of the Holy Spirit of God, as an advocate and a representative of the supreme sovereign power of God. The Holy Spirit instructs, corrects, and direct everything we engage our heart to do.

> *"For who is this that engaged his heart to approach unto me? Saith the Lord."*
> **Jer 30:21**

> *"For in him we live, and move, and have our being; as certain also of your own poets have said, For we are also his offspring."*
> **Acts 17:20**

> *"For it is God who is working in you, enabling you both to desire and to work out His good purpose."*
> **Phils 2:13**

Divine arrangement is simply the works of the Holy Spirit in our lives. Every believer must therefore yield to the leading, direction, correction, and instruction of the Holy Spirit.

Every time we operate in disobedience, we end up in frustration. We must embrace the Holy Spirit for a new beginning. You have led your self for a long time. embrace divine direction and enjoy rest and assurance the remaining days of your life. Whenever we yield to the leading of the Holy Spirit, we secure God's will and plan for our lives. Whenever we yield to sin we end up in frustration, and depression.

"There is a way which seemeth right unto a man, but the end thereof are the ways of death."
Proverb 14:12

One man once said, " No matter how long you go into the wrong direction in life, you will never get to your right destination in life." Like the above scripture says "there is a way which seemeth right...." often we find ourselves in the wrong career, marriage or job in life. Most people end up in the wrong profession, or do jobs, that are convenient for them, not because it is commanded by the Lord, but because it was convenient for them. As long as you are doing your own thing in life, it will always end up with struggle and frustration. I encourage you to embrace divine leading and live a free life the remaining days of your life.

Remember........

"Moreover whom he did predestinate, them he also called: and whom he called, them he also justified: and whom he justified, them he also glorified. What shall we then say to these things? If God be for us, who can be against us?"
Romans 8:30-31

Unless we understand how to confront challenges in life, we will forever be defeated by trials and obstacles.Jesus reassured us in John sixteen verse thirty three. It is written: *"These things I have spoken unto you, that in me ye might have peace. In the world ye shall have tribulation: but be of good cheer; I have overcome the world."* (John 16:33) We must therefore develop faith to confront and conquer any hardship or difficulty, facing our lives. As a believer, we must have faith to confront any challenge, or hardship, prevailing against us in life. As long as we stand by faith, all things will work out together for our good in life.

"And we know that all things work together for good to them that love God, to them who are the called according to his purpose."
Romans 8:28

Therefore, I pray as you read this book, no matter the challenges facing your life, it will work out for your good in the mighty name of Jesus.

HAPPY READING!

"And we know that all things work together for good to them that love God, to them who are the called according to his purpose."
Romans 8:28

HIS DESTINY WAS THE **CROSS....**

HIS PURPOSE WAS **LOVE.....**

HIS REASON WAS **YOU....**

SCRIPTURAL PRINCIPLES TO SECURE HEAVENLY BLESSING

"And seeing the multitudes, he went up into a mountain: and when he was set, his disciples came unto him, and he opened his mouth, and taught them, saying:

Blessed are the poor in spirit: for theirs is the kingdom of heaven.

Blessed are they that mourn: for they shall be comforted.

Blessed are the meek: for they shall inherit the earth.

Blessed are they which do hunger and thirst after righteousness: for they shall be filled.

Blessed are the merciful: for they shall obtain mercy.

Blessed are the pure in heart: for they shall see God.

Blessed are the peacemakers: for they shall be called the children of God.

Blessed are they which are persecuted for righteousness› sake: for theirs is the kingdom of heaven.

Blessed are ye, when men shall revile you, and persecute you, and shall say all manner of evil against you falsely, for my sake.

Rejoice, and be exceeding glad: for great is your reward in heaven: for so persecuted they the prophets which were before you."
Mathew 5:1-12

THE LAW OF RECEIVING

To receive, we must give, and to give, we must love.

"For God so loved the world that He gave......"
John3:16 It is written "Give, and it shall be given unto you; good measure, pressed down, and shaken together, and running over, shall men give into your bosom. For with the same measure that ye mete withal it shall be measured to you again."
Luke 6:38.

If we must receive in life, we must become givers ourselves. Jesus said it is more blessing to give than to receive. Every time we give, we position our life for power, breakthrough, and for next level.

"But as many as received him, to them gave he power to become the sons of God, even to them that believe on his name:"
John1:12

HOW DO I GIVE?

1) We give cheerfully to God (2 Cor 9:7)
2) We give willingly to God (1 Cor 9:17, Exodus 35:5-22)
3) We give righteously to God (Mal 3:3)
4) We give in faith to God (Eccl 11:1)
5) We give in love to God. (1 King 3:3, John 3:16)
6) We give liberally to God (Proverb 11:25, Proverb 28:27)
7) We give to God for health and long life. (Psalm 41:1-3, Ps 91:16)
8) We give to support the kingdom of God. (Matthew 6:33)
9) We give our best, not left over. (Mal1:6-8, 2 Sam 24:24, Gen 8:20)

HIGHLIGHTS TO DIVINE ARRANGEMENT

----HAVE FAITH IN GOD----

In our life time there will be times of trial and tribulation but everyone who believes in divine arrangement must have faith in God.

"And Jesus answering saith unto them, Have faith in God."
Mark 11:22

Faith in God is all it takes for God to divinely arrange things ahead of us. It is written *" I will go before thee, and make the crooked places straight: I will break in pieces the gates of brass, and cut in sunder the bars of iron:"* (Isaiah 45:2)

What we call faith is not faith unless there is a corresponding action in what we are saying. Every one must therefore make their life reflect what they confess and believe in their heart. Often God train's us for endurance, accountability, responsibility, strength, wisdom, and speed by allowing us, to go through certain challenges in life. Even physical stamina does not develop with ease. If we must understand divine arrangement for our life, we must develop faith in God to access revelation, wisdom to drive God's plan and purpose and understanding about our own unique strength, threats, opportunities, and weakness in life.

We must always believe in God, even in times of trials and tribulation in our lives.

"These things I have spoken unto you, that in me ye might have peace. In the world ye shall have tribulation: but be of good cheer; I have overcome the world."
John16:33.

We are not exempted from trial and tribulation in life. But as faithful believers we must depend on God for all things and at all times. In times of trials we must hope in God for our vindication, deliverance, and protection against the harassment and assault of the enemy.

We must always obey and follow God's divine leading and direction in our lives.

Unless we obey God's leading we will never experience His supernatural treasure reserved for us all in life. We must develop faith not to fear any evil when things are not really in our favor in life.

"Yea, though I walk through the valley of the shadow of death, I will fear no evil: for thou art with me; thy rod and thy staff they comfort me."
Psalms 23:4

Every time we acknowledge the doing of the Lord in our lives, we come out of any prevailing predicament victorious in life. *"If ye be willing and obedient, ye shall eat the good of the land."* (Isaiah 1:19) As long as we can endure our trial times God will lead us in to our blessing in life. *"If they obey and serve him, they shall spend their days in prosperity, and their years in pleasures."* **Job 36:11**. Although it takes the fruit of the spirit called patience and endurance to overcome trial and temptation in life, we must never neglect or ignore the place of prayer in our lives.

PRAYER:

"And he spake a parable unto them to this end, that men ought always to pray, and not to faint;"
Luke 18:1

In my own understanding, prayer has no substitute in life. It is not an elective in life. Prayer is compulsory if we claim to believe in God. "Every time we travail in prayer in life, we prevail with answer." Unless you develop a prayer life, you are heading into frustration. When the bible says *"And this is the confidence that we have in him, that, if we ask any thing according to his will, he heareth us."* (1 John 5:14) This asking must be performed in a time of prayer. I pray you develop a prayer life and follow the hand of God over your life in Jesus Name.

God expects a disciplined and devoted prayer life from us all, if we must experience divine arrangement.

"He will not suffer thy foot to be moved: he that keepeth thee will not slumber. Behold, he that keepeth Israel shall neither slumber nor sleep. The Lord is thy keeper: the Lord is thy shade upon thy right hand.
Pslams 121:3-5

----*We Must live by faith*----

A life of faith is a life of obedience, and a life of obedience is a life of meekness, love and humility. We must be embrace faith without measures, from our heart if we must experience divine arrangement in life. God is obligated to bless us in life, because he is too faithful to fail.

" Faithful is he that calleth you, who also will do it."
Theo 5:24

PRAYER POINT TO BREAK THE STRONG HOLD

- Holy Spirit of God, frustrate and disappoint all my oppositions, in the name of Jesus.

- I break every forces of darkness militating against my future in the name of Jesus.

- I paralyze every spoken curse against my life, break, in the name of Jesus.

- I bled the blood of Jesus over every prevailing hindrance over my life in the name of Jesus.

- You inward curses, militating against my virtues, break, in the name of Jesus.

- I destroy every power working against my life in the name of Jesus.

- Let every spirit of Balaam hired to curse my progress, fall down and die, in the name of Jesus.

- Every curse that I have brought into my life through ignorance and disobedience, break by fire, in the name of Jesus.

- Every power magnetizing physical and spiritual curses to me, I raise the blood of Jesus against you and I challenge you by fire, in the name of Jesus.

- Father, Lord, turn all my self-imposed curses to blessings, in the name of Jesus.

- Every instrument, put in place to frustrate me become impotent, in the name of Jesus.

- I reject every cycle of frustration, in the name of Jesus.

- Every agent assigned to frustrate me, perish by fire, in the name of Jesus.

- Every power tormenting my life, die by the sword, in the name of Jesus.

- I destroy the power of every satanic arrest in my life, in the name of Jesus.

- All satanic-arresting agents, release me in the mighty name of our Lord Jesus Christ.

- Everything that is representing me in the demonic world against my career, be destroyed by the fire of God, in the name of Jesus.

- Spirit of the living God, quicken the whole of my being, in the name of Jesus.

- God, smash me and renew my strength, in the name of Jesus.

- Holy Spirit, open my eyes to see beyond the visible to the invisible, in the name of Jesus.

- Lord, ignite my career with Your fire.

- O Lord, liberate my spirit to follow the leading of the Holy Spirit.

- Holy Spirit, teach me to pray through problems instead of praying about, it in the name of Jesus.

- O Lord, deliver me from the lies I tell myself.

- Every evil spiritual padlock and evil chain hindering my success, be roasted, in the name of Jesus.

- I rebuke every spirit of spiritual deafness and blindness in my life, in the name of Jesus.

- O Lord, empower me to resist satan that he would flee.

- I chose to believe the report of the Lord and no other, in the name of Jesus.

- Lord, anoint my eyes and my ears that they may see and hear wondrous things from heaven.

- O Lord, anoint me to pray without ceasing.

- In the name of Jesus, I capture every power behind any career failure.

- Holy Spirit, rain on me now, in the name of Jesus.

- Holy Spirit, uncover my darkest secrets, in the name of Jesus.

- You spirit of confusion, loose your hold over my life, in the name of Jesus.

- In the power of the Holy Spirit, I defy satan's power upon my career, in the name of Jesus.

- Let water of life flush out every unwanted stranger in my life, in the name of Jesus.

- You the enemies of my career, be paralyzed, in the name of Jesus.

- O Lord, begin to clean away from my life all that does not reflect You.

- Holy Spirit fire, ignite me to the glory of God, in the name of Jesus.

- Oh Lord, let the anointing of the Holy Spirit break every yoke of backwardness in my life.

- I frustrate every demonic arrest over my spirit-man, in the name of Jesus.

- Let the blood of Jesus remove any unprogressive label from every aspect of my life, in Jesus' name.

- Anti-breakthrough decrees, be revoked, in the name of Jesus.

CHAPTER 1

WHAT IS DIVINE ARRANGEMENT?

"And we know that all things work together for good to them that love God, to them who are the called according to his purpose."
Romans 8:28

Divine arrangement means; the hand of God in the life of a man. If I may put it this way; Divine arrangement means God's way of doing things, and revealing things into our lives. Often it can be through a calling, career, or life experience. We are clearly admonished by the Holy scripture;

"For my thoughts are not your thoughts, neither are your ways my ways, saith the Lord. For as the heavens are higher than the earth, so are my ways higher than your ways, and my thoughts than your thoughts." (Isaiah 55:8-9)

For anyone to understand the plan and purpose of God concerning their lives we must seek the face of God in prayers and also search the Holy scripture. Late Dr. Myles Monroe once said and I quote, *"when the purpose of a thing is not known, abuse is inevitable."*

GOD'S PLAN AND THOUGHT ARE GOOD TOWARDS US IN LIFE

" For I know the thoughts that I think toward you, saith the Lord, thoughts of peace, and not of evil, to give you an expected end."
Jer 29:11

It is always difficult for us to accept God's leading in our lives especially when the challenge and experiences are harsh to us. Often times God will allow us to be exposed to certain prevailing challenges, just to prepare us for the next awaiting blessing and promotion. It is written *"And it came to pass, when Pharaoh had let the people go, that God led them not through the way of the land of the Philistines, although that was near; for God said, Lest peradventure the people repent when they see war, and they return to Egypt."* (Exodus 13:17)

Often God wants us to be tested before we can be trusted in life. Unless you have been through physical pain, it will be difficulty for you to relate to anyone in physical pain. Job said *"But he knoweth the way that I take: when he hath tried me, I shall come forth as gold."* (Job 23:10) One of the primary reasons why God does not allow certain desires to come into our lives right now, is because we cannot handle it now. It is written *"I have yet many things to say unto you, but ye cannot bear them now."* (John 16:12)

GOD REWARDS US ACCORDING TO OUR DOING.

It is written *"Great in counsel, and mighty in work: for thine eyes are open upon all the ways of the sons of men: to give every one according to his ways, and according to the fruit of his doings"* (Jer 32:19)

God takes consideration to what we can do, experience, see and handle in life, before releasing anything into our lives.

GOD SEARCHES OUR HEART

It is written *"For the eyes of the Lord run to and fro throughout the whole earth, to shew himself strong in the behalf of them whose heart is perfect toward him. Herein thou hast done foolishly: therefore from henceforth thou shalt have wars."* (2 Chronicle 16:9).

As long as our heart is not pure, God will continue to deal with us based on the purity of our conscience. There are some financial blessing that will not come to certain people because they will use it for evil and for destruction.

" I the Lord search the heart, I try the reins, even to give every man according to his ways, and according to the fruit of his doings."
Jer 17:10

GOD PONDERS OUR HEART

"....but the Lord pondereth the hearts."
Proverb 21:2

Most of us live life the way we do, because we lack the understanding of God's love for us. We must always recognize that God's love for us, is "unconditional". It is not based on merit, none of us deserve it. Unless we understand the love of God for our lives, we will never become conquerors in life. It will be inevitable for us to do all things in Christ Jesus. God's love for us is a mystery, that is powerful beyond our comprehension. That is why He ponders our heart to see if we love him back. If you care only for yourself and family, and do not care about the Kingdom of God (the house of God- your local church), you do not love God.

Every time there is a delay in our life, it does not mean that it is not in God's plan. We must always wait for our appointed time in life. Although it is the will of God, for us to prosper in life, often God allows us to experience certain challenges in life to prepare you for the prosperity. If God blesses you today can you handle it? After David experienced frustration at the hand of King Saul, He said *"And in my prosperity I said, I shall never be moved."* (Psalm 30:6) It is written *"And it came to pass, when Pharaoh had let the people go, that God led them not through the way of the land of the Philistines, although that was near; for God said, Lest peradventure the people repent when they see war, and they return to Egypt."* (Exodus 13:17)

Divine arrangement is the will of God. Delay does not mean denial in life. We must always trust God, and put our faith in God, regardless of the present predicament in life."…..for he hath said, I will never leave thee, nor forsake thee." Hebrews13:5. God is never late, God is always on time. *"When my father and my mother forsake me, then the Lord will take me up."* (Psalm 27:10)

NEVER QUESTION GOD WHEN THINGS ARE NOT GOING RIGHT FOR YOU.

ONLY BELIEVE

It is written "Howbeit in the business of the ambassadors of the princes of Babylon, who sent unto him to enquire of the wonder that was done in the land, God left him, to try him, that he might know all that was in his heart." (2 Chr 32:31) Often God will not only ponder our heart but test our faith in Him. The fact that every thing is not working out for you the way you planned it does not mean the hand of the Lord is not upon your life. Some church folks question the Lord, why me, why Lord? I admonish you never question your maker lest you procure a curse. We are advised by the scripture "Woe unto him that striveth with his Maker! Let the potsherd strive with the potsherds of the earth. Shall the clay say to him that fashioneth it, What makest thou? or thy work, He hath no hands?" (Isaiah 45:9)

----WE PROVOKE DIVINE JUDGMENT BY OUR ACTION----

--King Saul and David--

Although King Saul wanted David dead, it was the will of God for David to become the next king of Israel. King Saul plotted so much evil against David, but the Spirit of the Lord was with David. God judged King Saul evil actions against David. That is why despite all the fame and reign of King Saul, when He died the bible recorded that it was as if he was never anointed. *"....for there the shield of the mighty is vilely cast away, the shield of Saul, as though he had not been anointed with oil."* (2 Samuel 1:21) We must always have a positive and a righteous mentality in life. God will eventually judge our action one day. Even when you believe you have been attacked in life, always bring before God in prayers. If we wish people around us well, God will judge us well.

--Haman and Mordecai--

God judged the evil action of Haman who wanted to wipe out all the Jews in those days. *"So they hanged Haman on the gallows that he had prepared for Mordecai. Then was the king's wrath pacified."* (Esther 7:10)

Often those who do not know God claim things just happen. That scripture says *"Before I formed thee in the belly I knew thee; and before thou camest forth out of the womb I sanctified thee, and I ordained thee a prophet unto the nations."* (Jer1:5). God knows everyone of us. Big and small. He called us all with His Holy calling.

"Who hath saved us, and called us with an holy calling, not according to our works, but according to his own purpose and grace, which was given us in Christ Jesus before the world began."
Tim 1:9

"According as his divine power hath given unto us all things that pertain unto life and godliness, through the knowledge of him that hath called us to glory and virtue:"
2 Peter 1:3

"Whereby are given unto us exceeding great and precious promises: that by these ye might be partakers of the divine nature, having escaped the corruption that is in the world through lust."
2 Peter 1:4

"Moreover whom he did predestinate, them he also called: and whom he called, them he also justified: and whom he justified, them he also glorified."
Romans 8:30

WHAT ARE THE HINDRANCES TO DIVINE ARRANGEMENT

Unbelief:

All unbelievers hinders God plan and pattern for their lives. As long as we do not belief, we will never experience the hand of God.

Fear of the unknown

What is fear?

F.........FALSE

E...................EXPERIENCE

A......................................APPEARING

R...REAL

Another interpretation of fear

F.........FACELESS

E......................ENEMY

A......................................AFFLICTING

R...REASONING

Another interpretation of fear

F………..FREQUENTLY

E………………….EXPECTED

A……………………………….ADVARSITY

R………………………………………………..REALIZED

Another interpretation of fear

F……………..FANTASIZED

E……………………….EXAGGERATION

A………………………………………….ABOVE

R……………………………………………………..REALITY

Another interpretation of fear

F………….FIERCE

E…………………..EMOTION

A……………………………….AROUSING

R…………………………………………….RESTLESSNESS

Another interpretation of fear

 F............FAILURE

 E......................EXPECTED

 A..AND

 R...REHEARSED

Another interpretation of fear

 F..........FACELESS

 E......................EXPRESSION

 A....................................ACKNOWLEDGED

 R..REPEATEDLY

Living in sin

As long as we live in sin, the blessing of the Lord upon our lives will be far fetch from us. It is written. *"Wherefore come out from among them, and be ye separate, saith the Lord, and touch not the unclean thing; and I will receive you."* (2 Cor 6:17). Unless we confess and forsake our sins, we will never experience the hand of God.

----Bitterness of the heart----

It is written *"Looking diligently lest any man fail of the grace of God; lest any root of bitterness springing up trouble you, and thereby many be defiled."* (Hebrew 12:15)

God is a spirit and not a man. As long as we pretend outwardly, God searches and rewards us based on our conscience. It is written *"And herein do I exercise myself, to have always a conscience void to offence toward God, and toward men."* (Acts 24:16)

----We must all repent of every sin----

We are told "He heareth not sinners" (John 9:31) Unless we come out of sin, we will never taste righteousness and real liberty in life. If we must experience divine arrangement in our life time we must repent and follow the ways and knowledge of God. *"Wherefore seeing we also are compassed about with so great a cloud of witnesses, let us lay aside every weight, and the sin which doth so easily beset us, and let us run with patience the race that is set before us."* (Hebrew 12:1)

As people of God, we must be conscious of divine arrangement in our lives, especially when every thing is prevailing against us in life. God expects us to be faithful especially in times of trials. It is written *" Faithful is he that calleth you, who also will do it."* (Theo5:24)

WHAT DO I DO TO UNDERSTAND DIVINE ARRANGEMENT

----We must be pure in our hearts----

"Unto the pure all things are pure: but unto them that are defiled and unbelieving is nothing pure; but even their mind and conscience is defiled."
Titus 1:15

It takes purity of heart to hear the heart bits of God. It takes purity of heart to understand what God has in stock for us in life. It is written "Blessed are the pure in heart: for they shall see God."
Mathew 5:8

Remember.......

"How much more shall the blood of Christ, who through the eternal Spirit offered himself without spot to God, purge your conscience from dead works to serve the living God?"
Hebrew 9:14

Unless we are pure from the inside of our heart we shall never comprehend the mysteries of divine arrangement in life.

----*We must practice righteousness*---

"Blessed are they which do hunger and thirst after righteousness: for they shall be filled.
Mathew 5:6

Unless we embrace righteousness and praiseful in life, we shall forever walk in darkness. *"Give glory to the Lord your God, before he cause darkness, and before your feet stumble upon the dark mountains, and, while ye look for light, he turn it into the shadow of death, and make it gross darkness."* (Jer 13:16) It is written, *".....he that doeth righteousness is righteous, even as he is righteous."* (1 John 3:7)

------*We must be peace maker*------

. *"Blessed are the peacemakers: for they shall be called the children of God."*
Mathew 5:9

----*We must be merciful*----

The acts of mercy is a virtue that comes from the heart of every believer. As believers we must prove the dignity of our Christianity by showing mercy to all. Until we learn and embrace the act of showing mercy to others we will not gain genuine strength, power, and authority in life.

"Blessed are the merciful: for they shall obtain mercy."
Mathew 5:7

----*We must love our neighbours as ourselves*----

"For God so loved the world, that he gave his only begotten Son, that whosoever believeth in him should not perish, but have everlasting life."
John 3:16

God expects us to show love from a genuine heart to everyone around us. Jesus said *"Thou shalt love thy neighbour as thyself"* (Mathew 22:39). *"And we have known and believed the love that God hath to us. God is love; and he that dwelleth in love dwelleth in God, and God in him."* (1 John 4:16)

----*We must be meek in life*----

God does not release His power to any proud man/woman. Until we are humbled and meek in life, we will never experience His presence that comes with fullness of joy. Remember that at His right hand is pleasures for us all for evermore. One of the greatest secret of Moses greatness was hidden in meekness. It is written, *"Now the man Moses was very meek, above all the men which were upon the face of the earth."* (Number 12:3)

Moses became the greatest as a result of the genuine meekness. I encourage you today to humble yourself before all men, and God will exalt you in due time. *"And there arose not a prophet since in Israel like unto Moses, whom the Lord knew face to face."* (Deut 34:10)

What must I do going forward?

"Examine yourselves, whether ye be in the faith; prove your own selves. Know ye not your own selves, how that Jesus Christ is in you, except ye be reprobates?"
2 Cor 13:5

We must consciously do away with every outward sin in our lives. The book of Galatian summarized for us all outward sin in life.

"Now the works of the flesh are manifest, which are these; Adultery, fornication, uncleanness, lasciviousness, Idolatry, witchcraft, hatred, variance, emulations, wrath, strife, seditions, heresies, Envyings, murders, drunkenness, revelings, and such like: of the which I tell you before, as I have also told you in time past, that

they which do such things shall not inherit the kingdom of God." (Gal 5:20-22)

How do I come out of sin?

It is written *"....Repent, and be baptized every one of you in the name of Jesus Christ for the remission of sins, and ye shall receive the gift of the Holy Ghost.* (Acts 2:38)

To come out of sin first, we must repent. Repentance is the first step into healing and deliverance. We will never experience genuine power and encounter His presence unless we genuinely repent of our sins. *"If we confess our sins, he is faithful and just to forgive us our sins, and to cleanse us from all unrighteousness."* (1 John 1:9)

Whenever we repent we position ourselves to receive His power.

"But as many as received him, to them gave he power to become the sons of God, even to them that believe on his name:"
John 1:12

We must confess Jesus as the Lord over our life.

We must confess with our mouth that Jesus is Lord. *" For with the heart man believeth unto righteousness; and with the mouth confession is made unto salvation."* (Romans 10:10)

Acknowledge

We acknowledge we are all sinners, and that He died for our sake. (Rom 3:23) We must repent of our sins. We must repent of our sins. (Acts 3:19, Luke 13:5, 2 Peter 3:9) We must believe in God.

We must believe in God for us to experience power, authority, and strength. *"But as many as received him, to them gave he power to become the sons of God, even to them that believe on his name:"* (John 1:12)

How to provoke the Power of the Holy Ghost

----Believe in the ministry of the Holy Spirit----

For us to encounter the power and presence of the Holy Spirit, we must believe in Him and in His ministry.

----Acknowledge the person of the Holy Spirit----

We must always recognize the voice of the Holy Spirit in our lives.

----Believe in the ministration of the Holy Spirit----

If we must provoke divine alignment in life, we must submit to the ministration of the Holy Spirit. We must have a relationship that will culminate in fellowship with the person of the Holy Spirit.

----Submit & obey the person of the Holy Spirit----

We must always seek for the divine guidance of the Holy Spirit in our lives

----Welcome the supernatural presence of the Holy Spirit----

We must welcome and appreciate the supernatural presence of the Holy Spirit in our lives

"Even the Spirit of truth; whom the world cannot receive, because it seeth him not, neither knoweth him: but ye know him; for he dwelleth with you, and shall be in you. I will not leave you comfortless: I will come to you." (John 14:17-18)

If we must understand divine arrangement upon our lives we must come to know the Holy Spirit. We must embrace the doing of the Holy Spirit in our lives. *"For it is God which worketh in you both to will and to do of his good pleasure."* (Phil 2:13)

DECISION KEYS

1) NOTHING CHANGES UNTIL YOU MAKE UP YOUR MIND

2) DECISION IS THE GATEWAY TO DELIVERANCE.

3) UNTIL YOU DECIDE, NO ONE WILL DECIDE FOR YOU.

4) YOUR PROSPERITY IS PROPORTIONAL TO YOUR DECISIONS.

5) THE DECISION YOU MAKE WILL DETERMINE THE FUTURE YOU WILL CREATE

6) DECISION CREATES FUTURE & FULFILLS DESTINIES.

7) DECISION BEAUTIFIES OUR FUTURE.

8) DECISION KEEPS YOU OUT OF TROUBLE

9) DECISION EXEMPTS YOU FROM EVIL

10) DECISION GUARANTEES ETERNITY

11) YOU CAN ONLY GO FAR IN LIFE BY YOUR FAITH DECISIONS.

12) YOU ARE POOR BECAUSE YOU MADE SUCH DECISIONS

13) MAKE A DECISION & CHANGE YOUR LIFE.

14) LIFE CHANGING DECISIONS IS A FUNCTION OF QUALITY INFORMATION

15) SUCCESS IN LIFE IS A FUNCTION OF DECISION.

16) LIFE EXPERIENCES IS FULL OF DECISIONS.

17) DECISIONS CHANGES DESTINIES.

18) NEVER SETTLE FOR INFORMATION ONLY LOOK FOR REVELATION

19) YOU ARE WHERE YOU ARE TODAY BASED ON YOUR LAST DECISION.

20) INFORMATION IS CRUCIAL IN DECISION MAKING

21) DECISION MAKERS RULE THE WORLD.

22) YOU CAN RULE YOUR WORLD BY QUALITY DECISIONS

23) AS LONG AS YOU DECIDE RIGHTLY SATAN CANNOT HARASS YOU.

CHAPTER 2

PARTNERSHIP WITH THE HOLY SPIRIT

"But ye shall receive power, after that the Holy Ghost is come upon you, and ye shall be witnesses unto me both in Jerusalem, and in all Judea, and in Samaria, and unto the uttermost part of the earth."
Acts 1:8

The Holy Spirit is our senior partner, and unless we embrace His leading we will not accomplish much in life. Every time we embrace the holy spirit God grants us power to subdue and the Holy spirit directs our path. *"And, behold, I send the promise of my Father upon you: but tarry ye in the city of Jerusalem, until ye be endued with power from on high."* (Luke 24:49)

We will not go far in life unless we embrace the Holy Spirit. We must establish a relationship, and fellowship with Him, if we must be divinely guided in life. Partnership with the Holy Spirit is all it takes for us to provoke divine plan for our lives. We must always acknowledge the presence of God in our lives. Partnership with the Holy Spirit is a two way mutual communication and understanding. We must therefore recognize Him in our life and allow Him to lead us into our bless in life. Our breakthrough in life might take time, but it will take God. *"For the vision is yet for an appointed time, but at the end it shall speak, and not lie: though it tarry, wait for it; because it will surely come, it will not tarry."* (Habakkuk 2:3)

WHAT DO I MEAN BY PARTNERSHIP WITH THE HOLY SPIRIT?

Partnership with the Holy Spirit means know what God is doing in our lives per time. God is constantly doing something new in our lives. It is our ability to recognize it that enhances it to move faster for us.

Partnership with the Holy Spirit is the plat form for dominion, power, and authority. Unless we come to know him, and knowing him means encountering His power and presence, we will never accomplish greater task in life. God has called us but we must be engrafted and filled with the Holy Ghost before we can comfortably launch out in any area of life. *"And they were all filled with the Holy Ghost and began to speak with other tongues, as the Spirit gave them utterance."* (Acts 2:4)

Partnership with the Holy Spirit is the access key into breakthrough and promotion in life. We all desire breakthrough and promotion in life, but until we join force with the Holy Spirit, we will forever live in defeat and fear.

HOW DO I PARTNER WITH THE HOLY SPIRIT?

----WALKING IN THE SPIRIT----

"This I say then, Walk in the Spirit, and ye shall not fulfill the lust of the flesh."
Gal 5:16

For us to partner with the Holy Spirit we must embrace walking and communicating in the spirit. Every time we walk in the spirit we receive deeper revelation about the person of the Holy Spirit.

"If we live in the Spirit, let us also walk in the Spirit."
Gal 5:25

----WALK IN AGREEMENT----

Unless we are in agreement with the Holy spirit, we lose His presence. *"Can two walk together, except they both agreed?"* (Amos 3:3)

----WALK IN LOVE----

Every time we walk in love, we literally walk in God. *"...God is love; and he that dwelleth in love dwelleth in God, and God in him"* (1 John 4:16)

----WALK IN TRUTH----

Whenever we walk in truth, we walk in God. *"Jesus saith unto him, I am the way, the truth, and the life: no man cometh unto the Father, but by me."* (John 14:6)

Whenever we walk in truth, we walk in freedom. It is written *"And ye shall know the truth, and the truth shall make you free."* (John 8:32)

Whenever we walk in truth we walk in revelation of God *"Howbeit when he, the Spirit of truth, is come, he will guide you into all truth: for he shall not speak of himself; but whatsoever he shall hear, that shall he speak: and he will shew you things to come."* (John 16:13)

----FAITH----

It takes faith to hear and partnership with Holy Spirit of God. *" We having the same spirit of faith, according as it is written, I believed, and therefore have I spoken; we also believe, and therefore speak."* (2 Cor 4:13)

----*PRAY ALWAYS*----

- Confess, forsake and renounce all our sins.

- Purify yourself with the blood of Jesus.

- Ask for the power of the Holy Spirit to come upon us.

- Forgive all those who have offended us and ask for forgiveness from all those we offended.

- Fast and pray often.

Prayer to provoke Divine Mercy & Timely Intervention

- Lord open our spiritual ears and eyes in the name of Jesus!

- Forgive our sins Lord, as we forgive those who trespass against us.

- And do not lead us into temptation.

- But deliver us from evil.

- Lord if we have abandoned your will for our lives, have mercy on us and forgive us in Jesus name!

- Lord show us your purpose for our lives, in Jesus name!

- Lord Jesus we come before you now, forgive us our sins.

- Come into our lives and take control of our lives in Jesus name we pray.

- Lord deliver us from spiritual ignorance in Jesus name Amen!

- Let Your will be done on earth O Lord, as it is in heaven, in Jesus name!

- You are holy, holy, Lord God Almighty, who was and is and is to come, Amen!

- Every evil spiritual gate confronting our lives be destroyed like the walls of Jericho, in the name of Jesus!

- Lord let there be restoration of all that we've lost at the midnight hour, in Jesus name!

- At midnight, I will rise and give thanks to You, because of Your righteous judgments. (Ps. 119:62)

- Lord let there be restoration of lost time, opportunities, health, blessings, prosperity, favour and spiritual in filling according to your will and purpose for our lives in Jesus name we prayer Amen!

- Is not your word like a fire O Lord? And like a hammer that breaks the rock in pieces? (Jer. 23:29)

- I have been crucified with Christ; it is no longer I who live, but Christ lives in me; and the life I now live in the flesh I live by faith in the Son of God, who loved me and gave himself for me. (Gal. 2:20).

- Lift up your hands O you gates! And be lifted up, you everlasting doors! And the King of glory shall come in. Who is this King of glory? The Lord strong and mighty, The Lord mighty in battle. (Ps. 24:7-8)

- He has broken the gates of brass, and cuts the bars of iron in sunder. (Ps. 107:16)

- You are holy, holy, Lord God Almighty, who was and is and is to come, Amen!

- Lord let the heavens cooperate with us now, in the heavens, water and land in the name of Jesus!

- Lord let the earth reject evil instructions against us, in the name of Jesus!

- We put on the Lord Jesus and we make no provision for the flesh, in Jesus name.

- The thief does not come except to steal, to kill and to destroy. Jesus came that we should have life, and that we may have it more abundantly. (John 10:10)

- Therefore we command the stars into war; O heavens fight for us, in the name of Jesus!

- You are holy, holy, Lord God Almighty, who was and is and is to come, Amen!

- I reject any form of spiritual sleep, in the name of Jesus!

- Untie O Lord all evil principalities tied up in our family lines, in Jesus name!

- You are holy, holy, Lord God Almighty, who was and is and is to come, Amen!

- Let us O Lord utter our prayers in blood, sweat and tears, in Jesus name!

- Lord open our understanding, in the name of Jesus!

- You are holy, holy, Lord God Almighty, who was and is and is to come, Amen!

- It is written; do not be afraid of sudden terror; nor of the trouble from the wicked when it comes; for the Lord will be your confidence. And will keep your foot from being caught. (Prov. 3:26)

- Therefore, O Lord, cover us and our loved ones from the activities of terrorists, in Jesus name!

- It is written; avenge me of my adversary. (Lk. 18:3)

- Therefore, O Lord, arise and avenge us of all my adversaries in the name of Jesus!

- It is written; they fought from the heavens; the stars from their courses fought against Sisera. (Jud. 5:20)

- Therefore O heavens, fight for us in Jesus name!

- It is written; I will purge the rebels from among you, and those who transgress against Me; I will bring them out of the country where they dwell, but they shall not enter the land of Israel. They will know that I am the Lord. (Ezek. 20:38)

- Therefore, O Lord, purge and sanitize our household in the name of Jesus!

- It is written; then it was so, after all your wickedness – "woe, woe to you!" says the Lord God. (Ezek. 16:23)

- Therefore, woe unto all the vessels that the enemy is using to do us harm in the name of Jesus!

- It is written; behold therefore, I stretch out My hand against you, admonished your allotment, and gave you up to the will of those who hate you. (Ezek. 16:27)

- Therefore, let our enemies be delivered into the hands of their enemies in Jesus name!

- It is written; you shall be for fuel of fire; your blood shall be in the midst of the land. You shall not be remembered, for I the Lord have spoken. (Ezek. 21:32)

- Therefore, let all our spiritual enemies become fuel for divine fire in Jesus name!

- It is written; then they will know that I am the Lord, when I have set a fire in Egypt and all her helpers are destroyed. (Ezek. 30:8)

- Therefore, O Lord, let all the helpers of our enemies be destroyed in the name of Jesus.

- It is written; and the people to whom they prophesy shall be cast out in the streets of Jerusalem because of the famine and the sword; they will have no one to bury them – them nor their wives, their sons nor their daughters – for I will pour their wickedness on them. (Jer. 14:16)

- Therefore, O Lord, pour the wickedness of those who seek to destroy us upon their own heads in the name of Jesus!

- It is written; call together the archers against Babylon. All you who bend the bow encamp against it all around; let none of them escape. Repay her according to her work; According to all she has done, do to her; for she has been poured against the Lord, against the Holy one of Israel . (Jer. 50:29)

- Therefore, let all the hosts of the Lord turn against our spiritual enemies in Jesus name!

- It is written; let God arise, let His enemies be scattered; let those also who hate him flee before him. (Ps. 68:1)

- Therefore, O God, arise and let all your enemies in our lives be scattered in Jesus name.

CHAPTER 3

COVENANT CONNECTIONS

"My covenant will I not break, nor alter the thing that is gone out of my lips."
Psalms 89:34

There are some special individuals that God has divinely arranged for our breakthrough and promotion in life. These men and women are those I called covenant connectors. Covenant connection are men and women of supernatural turn around. They are our God designed agents of change. Some people say it luck or it just happened but I submit to you that all things work together for our good.

They are men/women of favor planted by the spirit of God for our lifting and assistance in life. These men/women are our covenant connections. I call them divine accelerators, once we come into contact with them they pave the way for our breakthrough and blessing in life.

Although he came into Potiphar house as a slave but once Joseph entered that family, everything about Potiphar changed for good. *"...that the Lord blessed the Egyptian's house for Joseph's sake; and the blessing of the Lord was upon all that he had in the house, and in the field."* (Genesis 39:5)

Laban never experienced breakthrough in his cattle business, and in his family life, until he came into contact with Jacob, *"...I pray thee, if I have found favour in thine eyes, tarry: for I have learned by experience that the Lord hath blessed me for thy sake."* (Genesis 30:27).

Promotion & breakthrough becomes cheap and easy in life every time we locate our covenant connection in life. *"...I am the God of Abraham thy father: fear not, for I am with thee, and will bless thee, and multiply thy seed for my servant Abraham's sake."* (Genesis 26:24)

Our God covenant connection can be anywhere around us in life. We must be open, willing, and look out for them. There are times in life that our covenant connection is through our spouse (either wife or husband), although some of us live in denial, until the enemy penetrates into such relationship. What I am saying is, there is someone created by God to favor and help change our lifestyle. It must not be your operation supervisor at work, or the human resource manager, or your relative working with the federal governement. As familiar as your friend can be to you, it can be even your spouse, brother, uncle or auntie. God can use anybody for me and you.

"Thus saith the Lord; If ye can break my covenant of the day, and my covenant of the night, and that there should not be day and night in their season; Then may also my covenant be broken with David my servant, that he should not have a son to reign upon his throne; and with the Levites the priests, my ministers.

As the host of heaven cannot be numbered, neither the sand of the sea measured: so will I multiply the seed of David my servant, and the Levites that minister unto me.
Moreover the word of the Lord came to Jeremiah, saying,

Considerest thou not what this people have spoken, saying, The two families which the Lord hath chosen, he hath even cast them off? thus they have despised my people, that they should be no more a nation before them.

Thus saith the Lord; If my covenant be not with day and night, and if I have not appointed the ordinances of heaven and earth;

Then will I cast away the seed of Jacob and David my servant, so that I will not take any of his seed to be rulers over the seed of Abraham, Isaac, and Jacob: for I will cause their captivity to return, and have mercy on them." (Jer 33:20-26)

Our Lord God is a covenant keeping God. God out of favor divinely arrange and program certain men/women of distinction for our lifting and rising in life. As long as it's Gods divine arrangement for our lives, God will use any man/woman he chooses to use to bring to pass his good acts upon our lives.

WHAT ARE WE SAYING?

Unless we locate our covenant connectors we will ever remain in want of all things in life. I call these men/women point of contacts. Some fellows say it does not happen in America, that it only happens in Africa. But I prove you wrong. Who you know in life matters everywhere. Perhaps you have struggled without a job for a very long time because you do not know any one I prophesy to you that since you know your God he will make away for you in the mighty name of Jesus

----*ABRAM CONNECTED LOT*----

"And Lot also, which went with Abram, had flocks, and herds, and tents."
Genesis 13:5

---- JACOB CONNECTED LABAN----

"And Laban said unto him, I pray thee, if I have found favour in thine eyes, tarry: for I have learned by experience that the Lord hath blessed me for thy sake."
Genesis 30:27

----JOSEPH CONNECTED POTIPHAR THE EGYPTIANS-----

"And it came to pass from the time that he had made him overseer in his house, and over all that he had, that the Lord blessed the Egyptian's house for Joseph's sake; and the blessing of the Lord was upon all that he had in the house, and in the field."
Genesis 39:5

----Biblical point of contacts that helped some biblical characters.

David

David needed a point of contact to pursue, overtake and recover all that the Amalekites had taken away from him. David need this point of contact for total restoration.

*"And they found an Egyptian in the field, and brought him to David, and gave him bread, and he did eat; and they made him drink water; And they gave him a piece of a cake of figs, and two clusters of raisins: and when he had eaten, his spirit came again to him: for he had eaten no bread, nor drunk any water, three days and three nights. And David said unto him, To whom belongest thou? and whence art thou? And he said, **I am a young man of Egypt, servant to an Amalekite**; and my master left me, because three days agone I fell sick. We made an invasion upon the south of the Cherethites, and upon the coast which belongeth to Judah, and upon the south of Caleb; and we burned Ziklag with fire. And David said to him, Canst thou bring me down to this company? And he said, Swear unto me by God, that thou wilt neither kill me, nor deliver me into the hands of my master, and I will bring thee down to this company.*
(1Samuel 30:11-15)

Naaman-- The Syrian Solider

When Naaman the Syrian solider was plagued with leprosy, he needed a point of contact for his healing. If the little house maid did not reveal Elisha the man of God to Naaman the Syrian. Naaman would have died of the disease of leprosy.

"Now Naaman, captain of the host of the king of Syria, was a great man with his master, and honourable, because by him the Lord had given deliverance unto Syria: he was also a mighty man in valour, but he was a leper. And the Syrians had gone out by companies, and had brought away captive out of the land of Israel a little maid; and she waited on Naaman's wife. And she said unto her mistress, Would God my lord were with the prophet that is in Samaria! for he would recover him of his leprosy." (2 King 5:1-3)

Everything will work together for our good, but we must locate our point of contact. We must pray consciously, and ask God for revelation to meet in our life time, everyone designed by God to help reposition and usher us into our promotion and the breakthrough phase of our life.

However, we must not look up to man, neither must we put our trust in man. We must hope in God, put our trust in God. God will use anyone to change our life, according to His divine plan, and purpose concerning our lives. I pray you encounter all God position on your way for your lifting, promotion, and breakthrough in Jesus Mighty Name.

PRAYER POINT TO PROVOKE MY DIVINE ARRANGEMENT

I cancel my name and that of my family from the death register, with the fire of God, in the name of Jesus.

Every weapon of destruction fashioned against me and my family, be destroyed by the fire of God, in the name of Jesus.

Power of God, fight for me in every area of my life, in Jesus' name.

Every hindrance to my breakthrough, be melted by the fire of God, in the name of Jesus.

Every evil power against me, be scattered by the thunder fire of God, in the name of Jesus.

Father Lord, destroy every evil man/woman in the name of Jesus.

Every failures of the past, be converted to success , in Jesus' name.

Father Lord, let the former rain, the latter rain and Your blessing pour down on me now.

Father Lord, let all the failure turn into success for me, in the name of Jesus.

I receive power from on high and I paralyze all the powers of darkness that are diverting my blessings, in the name of Jesus.

Beginning from this day, I employ the services of the angels of God to open unto me every door of opportunity and breakthroughs, in the name of Jesus.

I will not go around in circles again, I will make progress, in the name of Jesus.

I shall not build for another to inhabit and I shall not plant for another to eat, in the name of Jesus.

I paralyse the powers of the emptier concerning my handiwork, in the name of Jesus.

O Lord, let every locust, caterpillar and palmerworm assigned to eat the fruit of my labour be roasted by the fire of God.

The enemy shall not spoil my testimony in this programme, in the name of Jesus.

By the blood of Jesus, I reject every backward journey, in the name of Jesus.

By the blood of Jesus, I paralyze every strongman attached to any area of my life, in the name of Jesus.

I pray, Let every agent of shame fashioned to

work against my life be paralyzed, in the name of Jesus.

I paralyse the activities of household wickedness over my life, in the name of Jesus.

I quench every strange fire emanating from evil tongues against me, in the name of Jesus.

Father Lord, give me power for maximum achievement.

Heavenly father, give me comforting authority to achieve my goal.

Blood of Jesus Christ, defend and fortify me with Your power.

I paralyse every spirit of disobedience in my life, in Jesus' name.

I refuse to disobey the voice of God, in the name of Jesus.

Every root of rebellion in my life, be uprooted, in Jesus' name.

By the blood of Jesus, I destroy every witchcraft spirit in my life, in the name of Jesus.

Contradicting forces promoting hindrance in my life, die, in Jesus' name.

Every inspiration of witchcraft in my family, be destroyed, in the name of Jesus.

Blood of Jesus, blot out every evil mark of witchcraft in my life, in the name of Jesus.

Every garment put upon me by witchcraft, be torn to pieces, in the name of Jesus.

Angels of God, begin to pursue my household enemies, let their ways be dark and slippery, in the name of Jesus.

Lord, confuse them and turn them against themselves.

By the blood of Jesus, I break every evil unconscious agreement with household enemies concerning my miracles, in the name of Jesus.

Household witchcraft, fall down and die, in the name of Jesus.

Father Lord, drag all the household wickedness to the Dead Sea and bury them there.

Father Lord, I reject to follow the evil pattern of remote control my household enemies.

My life, jump out from the cage of household wickedness, in the name of Jesus.

I command all my blessings and potentials buried by wicked household enemies to be exhumed, in the name of Jesus.

I will see the goodness of the Lord in the land of the living, in the name of Jesus.

Everything done against me to spoil my joy, receive destruction, in the name of Jesus.

Father Lord, as Abraham received favour in Your eyes, let me receive Your favour, so that I can excel in every area of my life.

Lord Jesus, help my shortcoming and infirmities in the name of Jesus.

It does not matter, whether I deserve it or not, I receive immeasurable favour from the Lord, in the name of Jesus.

By the blood of Jesus I receive every blessing God has apportioned to me in the name of Jesus.

My blessing will not be transferred to my neighbor in the name of Jesus.

Father Lord, disgrace every power that is tormenting my breakthrough in the name of Jesus.

Every step I take shall lead to outstanding success, in Jesus' name.

I shall prevail with man and with God in every area of my life, in the name of Jesus.

Every habitation of infirmity in my life, break to pieces, in the name of Jesus.

My body, soul and spirit, reject every evil load, in Jesus' name.

Evil foundation in my life, I pull you down today, in the mighty name of Jesus.

Every inherited sickness in my life, depart from me now, in the name of Jesus.

Every evil water in my body, get out, in the name of Jesus.

By the blood of Jesus, I cancel the effect of every evil dedication in my life, in the name of Jesus.

Holy Ghost fire, immunize my blood against satanic poisoning, in the name of Jesus.

Father Lord, put self control in my mouth, in the name of Jesus.

I refuse to get accustomed to sickness, in the name of Jesus.

Every door open to infirmity in my life, be permanently closed today, in the name of Jesus.

Every power contenting with God in my life, be roasted, in the name of Jesus.

Every power preventing God's glory from manifesting in my life, be paralysed, in the name of Jesus.

I loose myself from the spirit of desolation, in the name of Jesus.

Father Lord break me through in my home, in the name of Jesus.

Father Lord keep in me healthy, in the name of Jesus.

Father Lord break me through in my business, in the name of Jesus.

Let God be God in my economy, in the name of Jesus.

Glory of God, envelope every department of my life, in the name of Jesus.

The Lord that answereth by fire, be my God, in the name of Jesus.

By the blood of Jesus, all my enemies shall scatter to rise no more, in the name of Jesus.

Blood of Jesus, cry against all evil gatherings arranged for my sake, in the name of Jesus.

Father Lord, convert all my past failures to unlimited victories, in the name of Jesus.

Lord Jesus, create room for my advancement in every area of my life.

All evil thoughts against me, Lord turn them to be good for me.

Father Lord, give evil men for my life where evil decisions have been taken against me, in the name of Jesus.

Father Lord, advertise Your dumbfounding prosperity in my life.

Let the showers of dumbfounding prosperity fall in every department of my life, in the name of Jesus.

By the blood of Jesus, I claim all my prosperity in the name of Jesus.

Every door of my prosperity that has been shut, be opened now, in the name of Jesus.

Father Lord, convert my poverty to prosperity, in the name of Jesus.

Father Lord, convert my mistake to perfection, in the name of Jesus.

Father Lord, convert my frustration to fulfillment, in the name of Jesus.

Father Lord, bring honey out of the rock for me, in the name of Jesus.

By the blood of Jesus, I stand against every evil covenant of sudden death, in the name of Jesus.

By the blood of Jesus, I break every conscious and unconscious evil covenant of untimely death, in the name of Jesus.

You spirit of death and hell, you have no document in my life, in the name of Jesus.

You stones of death, depart from my ways, in the name of Jesus.

Father Lord, make me a voice of deliverance and blessing.

By the blood of Jesus, I tread upon the high places of the enemies, in the name of Jesus.

I bind and render useless, every blood sucking demon, in the name of Jesus.

You evil current of death, loose your grip over my life, in the name of Jesus.

By the blood of Jesus, I frustrate the decisions of the evil openers in my family, in the name of Jesus.

Fire of protection, cover my family, in the name of Jesus.

Father Lord, make my way perfect, in the name of Jesus.

Throughout the days of my life, I shall not be put to shame, in the name of Jesus.

By the blood of Jesus, I reject every garment of shame, in the name of Jesus.

By the blood of Jesus, I reject every shoe of shame, in the name of Jesus.

By the blood of Jesus, I reject every head-gear and cap of shame, in the name of Jesus.

Shamefulness shall not be my lot, in the name of Jesus.

Every demonic limitation of my progress as a result of shame, be removed, in the name of Jesus.

Every network of shame around me, be paralysed, in the name of Jesus.

Those who seek for my shame shall die for my sake, in the name of Jesus.

As far as shame is concerned, I shall not record any point for satan, in the name of Jesus.

In the name of Jesus, I shall not eat the bread of sorrow, I shall not eat the bread of shame and I shall not eat the bread of defeat.

No evil will touch me throughout my life, in the name of Jesus.

By the blood of Jesus, In every area of my life, my enemies will not catch me, in the name of Jesus.

By the blood of Jesus, In every area of my life, I shall run and not grow weary, I shall walk and shall not faint.

Father Lord, in every area of my life, let not my life disgrace You.

By the blood of Jesus, I will not be a victim of failure and I shall not bite my finger for any reason, in the name of Jesus.

Holy Spirit of God, Help me O Lord, to meet up with God's standard for my life.

By the blood of Jesus, I refuse to be a candidate to the spirit of amputation, in the name of Jesus.

By the blood of Jesus, with each day of my life, I shall move to higher ground, in the name of Jesus.

Every spirit of shame set in motion against my life, I bind you, in the name of Jesus.

Every spirit competing with my breakthroughs, be chained, in the name of Jesus.

By the blood of Jesus, I bind every spirit of slavery , in the name of Jesus.

By the blood of Jesus, In every day of my life, I disgrace all my stubborn pursuers, in the name of Jesus.

By the blood of Jesus, I bind, every spirit of Herod, in the name of Jesus.

Every spirit challenging my God, be disgraced, in Jesus' name.

Every Red Sea before me, be parted, in the name of Jesus.

By the blood of Jesus, I command every spirit of bad ending to be bound in every area of my life, in the name of Jesus.

By the blood of Jesus, Every spirit of Saul, be disgraced in my life, in the name of Jesus.

By the blood of Jesus, Every spirit of Pharaoh, be disgraced in my life, in Jesus' name.

By the blood of Jesus, I reject every evil invitation to backwardness, in Jesus' name.

By the blood of Jesus, I command every stone of hindrance in my life to be rolled away, in the name of Jesus.

Father Lord, roll away every stone of poverty from my life, in the name Jesus.

Let every stone of infertility in my marriage be rolled away, in the name of Jesus.

Let every stone of non-achievement in my life be rolled away, in the name of Jesus.

My God, roll away every stone of hardship and slavery from my life, in the name of Jesus.

My God, roll away every stone of failure planted in my life, my home and in my business, in the name of Jesus.

You stones of hindrance, planted at the edge of my breakthroughs, be rolled away, in the name of Jesus.

You stones of stagnancy, stationed at the border of my life, be rolled away, in the name of Jesus.

My God, let every stone of the 'amputator' planted at the beginning of my life, at the middle of my life and at the end of my life, be rolled away, in the name of Jesus.

Father Lord, I thank You for all the stones You have rolled away, I forbid their return, in the name of Jesus.

Let the power from above come upon me, in the name of Jesus.

Father Lord, advertise Your power in every area of my life, in the name of Jesus.

Father Lord, make me a power generator, throughout the days of my life, in the name of Jesus.

Let the power to live a holy life throughout the days of my life fall upon me, in the name of Jesus.

Let the power to live a victorious life throughout the days of my life fall upon me, in the name of Jesus.

Let the power to prosper throughout the days of my life fall upon me, in the name of Jesus.

Let the power to be in good health throughout the days of my life fall upon me, in the name of Jesus.

Let the power to disgrace my enemies throughout the days of my life fall upon me, in the name of Jesus.

Let the power of Christ rest upon me now, in the name of Jesus.

Let the power to bind and loose fall upon me now, in the name of Jesus.

Father Lord, let Your key of revival unlock every department of my life for Your revival fire, in the name of Jesus.

Every area of my life that is at the point of death, receive the touch of revival, in the name of Jesus.

Father Lord, send down Your fire and anointing into my life, in the name of Jesus.

Every uncrucified area in my life, receive the touch of fire and be crucified, in the name of Jesus.

Let the fire fall and consume all hindrances to my advancement, in the name of Jesus.

You stubborn problems in my life, receive the Holy Ghost dynamite, in the name of Jesus.

You carry-over miracle from my past, receive the touch of fire in the name of Jesus.

Holy Ghost fire, baptize me with prayer miracle, in Jesus' name.

By the blood of Jesus, Every area of my life that needs deliverance, receive the touch of fire and be delivered, in the name of Jesus.

Let my angels of blessing locate me now, in the name of Jesus.

Every satanic programme of impossibility, I cancel you now, in the name of Jesus.

Every household wickedness and its programme of impossibility, be paralysed, in the name of Jesus.

No curse will land on my head, in the name of Jesus.

Throughout the days of my life, I will not waste money on my health: the Lord shall be my healer, in the name of Jesus.

Throughout the days of my life, I will be in the right place at the right time.

Throughout the days of my life, I will not depart from the fire of God's protection, in the name of Jesus.

Throughout the days of my life, I will not be a candidate for incurable disease, in the name of Jesus.

Every weapon of captivity, be disgraced, in the name of Jesus.

Lord, before I finish this programme, I need an outstanding miracle in every area of my life.

Let every attack planned against the progress of my life be frustrated, in the name of Jesus.

I command the spirits of harassment and torment to leave me, in the name of Jesus.

Lord, begin to speak soundness into my mind and being.

I reverse every witchcraft curse issued against my progress, in the name of Jesus.

I condemn all the spirits condemning me, in the name of Jesus.

Let divine accuracy come into my life and operations, in the name of Jesus.

No evil directive will manifest in my life, in the name of Jesus.

Let the plans and purposes of heaven be fulfilled in my life, in the name of Jesus.

O Lord, bring to me friends that reverence Your name and keep all others away.

Let divine strength come into my life, in the name of Jesus.

Let every stronghold working against my peace be destroyed, in the name of Jesus.

Let the power to destroy every decree of darkness operating in my life fall upon me now, in the name of Jesus.

Lord, deliver my tongue from evil silence.

Lord, let my tongue tell others of Your life.

Lord, loose my tongue and use it for Your glory.

Lord, let my tongue bring straying sheep back to the fold.

Lord, let my tongue strengthen those who are discouraged.

Lord, let my tongue guide the sad and the lonely.

Lord, baptise my tongue with love and fire.

Let every unrepentant and stubborn pursuers be disgraced in my life, in the name of Jesus.

Let every iron-like curse working against my life be broken by the blood of Jesus, in the name of Jesus.

Let every problem designed to disgrace me receive open shame, in the name of Jesus.

Let every problem anchor in my life be uprooted, in Jesus' name.

Multiple evil covenants, be broken by the blood of Jesus, in the name of Jesus.

Multiple curses, be broken by the blood of Jesus, in Jesus' name.

Everything done against me with evil padlocks, be nullified by the blood of Jesus, in the name of Jesus.

Everything done against me at any cross-roads, be nullified by the blood of Jesus, in the name of Jesus.

Let every stubborn and prayer resisting demon receive stones of fire and thunder, in the name of Jesus.

Every stubborn and prayer resisting sickness, loose your evil hold upon my life, in the name of Jesus.

Every problem associated with the dead, be smashed by the blood of Jesus, in the name of Jesus.

I recover my stolen property seven fold, in the name of Jesus.

Let every evil memory about me be erased by the blood of Jesus, in the name of Jesus.

By the blood of Jesus, I disallow my breakthroughs from being caged, in Jesus' name.

Let the sun of my prosperity arise and scatter every cloud of poverty, in the name of Jesus.

I decree unstoppable advancement upon my life, in Jesus' name.

I soak every day of my life in the blood of Jesus and in signs and wonders, in the name of Jesus.

I break every stronghold of oppression in my life, in Jesus' name.

Let every satanic joy about my life be terminated, in the name of Jesus.

I paralyse every household wickedness, in the name of Jesus.

Let every satanic spreading river dry up by the blood of Jesus, in the name of Jesus.

I bind every ancestral spirit and command them to loose their hold over my life, in the name of Jesus.

CONCLUSION

"And we know that all things work together for good to them that love God, to them who are the called according to his purpose."
Romans 8:28

Believe us when we say these things, *"... all things work together for good to them that love God, to them who are the called according to his purpose.*

Our lives will remain plain unless we locate God's plan, and we will be battered and scattered in life, if we do not follow God's pattern.

WHAT ARE WE SAYING?

If we must activate divine plan and pattern over our lives, we must repent of our sinful ways, forsake them, and seek the face of the Lord forever more.

Divine plans means a living a life that is in the center of God's plan, fulfilling our glorious destiny. Often most single women always misinterpret divine plan to mean only their God ordained husband. I tell you divine plan means much more than husband. If you are single, I pray for a solution and answer to your God ordained spouse, if you are challenged with career crisis,

I pray you locate what God want you to do, and when He wants you to engage your self into it. If you are in the wrong business, I pray God reveal's His plan concerning your business for you. if you are looking for the fruit of the womb, I pray the Holy Spirit help you to conceive your bouncing baby in the Mighty Name of Jesus.

Divine arrangement deals with every area of our life. I therefore pray let all things work together for your good and according to His unique purpose concerning your life. *"For whom he did foreknow, he also did predestinate to be conformed to the image of his Son, that he might be the firstborn among many brethren. Moreover whom he did predestinate, them he also called: and whom he called, them he also justified: and whom he justified, them he also glorified."* (Romans 8:29-30)

Let us hear the conclusion of the whole matter: Fear God, and keep his commandments: for this is the whole duty of man.

For God shall bring every work into judgment, with every secret thing, whether it be good, or whether it be evil.
Eccl 12:13-14

If you are a born again Christian; we like to encourage you in your Christian life. If you are not a born again Christian we can help you here receive genuine salvation.

> *"Therefore if any man be in Christ, he is a new creature: old things are passed away; behold, all things are become new."*
> **2 Cor 5:17**

Now repeat this Prayer after me

Say Lord Jesus, I accept you today, as my Lord and my savior, forgive me of my sins wash me with your blood. Right now, I believe, I am sanctified, I am save, I am free, I am free from the Power of sin to serve the Lord Jesus. Thank you Lord for saving me. Amen.

Congratulations: YOU ARE NOW..

...A BORN AGAIN CHRISTIAN.

AGAIN I SAY TO YOU - CONGRATULATIONS!

What must I do to determine my divine visitation?

To determine divine visitation you must be born again! The word says as many as received him, to them gave He power to become the sons of God. Even to them that believe on his name.

To qualify for divine visitation, do the following sincerely

1) Acknowledge that you are a sinner and that He died for you. (Romans 3:23)

2) Repent of your sins. (Acts 3:19, Luke 13:5, 2 Peter 3:9)

3) Believe in your heart that Jesus died for your sin. (Romans 10:10)

4) Confess Jesus as the Lord over your life. (Romans 10:10, Acts 2:21)

Now repeat this Prayer after me

Say Lord Jesus, I accept you today, as my Lord and my savior, forgive me of my sins wash me with your blood. Right now, I believe, I am sanctified, I am save, I am free, I am free from the Power of sin to serve the Lord Jesus. Thank you Lord for saving me. Amen.

Congratulations: YOU ARE NOW...
...A BORN AGAIN CHRISTIAN.

AGAIN I SAY TO YOU - CONGRATULATIONS!

I adjure you to watch the Spirit of God bear witness with your Spirit confirming His word with signs following. The word says The Spirit itself beareth witness with our spirit, that we are the children of God. Join a bible believing church or join us on our weekly and Sunday worship services at 343 Sanford Avenue Newark New Jersey 07106.

WISDOM KEYS

1) Every Productive Society is a society heading to the top

2) Millions of Nigerians run away from Nigeria, very few Nigerians stay in Nigeria.

3) My decision to return Nigeria is the will of God for my life

4) My short coming in America after 18 years, trained me to be wise, to think, reflect and reason appropriately.

5) If you train your mind to reason it will train your hands to earn money.

6) It is absurd to use the money of the heathen to build the kingdom of the living God.

7) Every Ministry reveals its agenda and goal either at the beginning or at the end. Be careful of your life it is your first Ministry.

8) The average American mind is conditioned for a continual quest to get new things and (discard the former) and throw away old things.

9) When I considered well, my BMW jeep became my initial deposit for the work of the ministry in Nigeria

10) Money will never fall from any Treebank, Treasury Department or person. Make up your mind to be independent today.

11) Everyone is waiting for you to change your mind until you change your thinking nothing changes around you.

12) Multiple academic degrees in other discipline gave me the chance to think, reflect and reason

13) What so everyone are thinking and reflecting at the moment reveals you to the time and the now factor

14) All events and intents are the product of precise thought processes, accurate reason every event is designed for a designated timeline

15) Wisdom is your ability to think, to create and invent. If you can think wise enough you will come out of penury

16) The distance between you and success is your creative ability to think reason and reflect accurate.

17) Success is the result of hard work, commitment resolve and determination learning from past mistakes and failing.

18) If you organize your mind you have organized your life and destiny.

19) There is a thin line between success and failure. If you look above and beyond you are on your way to success.

20) Wealth is your ability to think, power is your ability to reason and success is your ability to be informed.

21) If you can make use of your mind by thinking and reasoning God will make use of your life and destiny.

22) Think and Be Great

23) Reflect, Reason, think and be great

24) Famous people are born of woman

25) That you will make it is your intention; that you will survive is your resolve, that you will succeed with changes is your determination, personal efforts and hard work.

26) No man was born a failure. Lack of vision is the end product of failure.

27) Working with mental patients encourages and aspire me to be a productive observant and dedicated to my assignment.

28) Successful people are not magicians, it is the will power combined with hard work, and determination and a resolve to succeed that

make them succeed.

29) In the unequivocal state of the mind, intention is not a location or a position it is the state of the mind.

30) So many people think that they think. The mind is used to think reflect and reason. You will remain blind with your eye open until you can see with your mind by thinking.

31) There is no favoritism in accurate and precise calculation

32) Although knowledge is power, information is the key and gateway to a great future.

33) It will take the hand of God to move the hand of man.

34) With the backing of the great wise God, nothing will disconnect you from your inheritance.

35) As long as you have wisdom and understanding of God, Satan and evil cannot manipulate your life and destiny.

36) You have come this far by yourself judgment and decision you have made in the past, now lean and listen to God for another dimension of greatness.

37) Great people are common people it is extra

ordinary effort and the price of sacrifice that produces greatness.

38) As a mental direct care worker I saw a great pastor and a motivational speaker within myself.

39) Menial job does not reduce your self-worth, until you resolve to achieve greatness see greatness in all you do; you will never count in your community.

40) The principle of Jesus will solve your gambling and addiction problems

41) The man of Jesus will lead you into heaven,

42) Everyone have their self-appraisal and what they think about you. Until you discover yourself other opinion about you will alter the real you.

43) Supervisors and directors are just a position in the chain of command in a work place. Never allow your supervisor hierarchy to alter your opinion about yourself.

44) Everyone can come out of debt if they make up their mind.

45) That I am not a decision maker at work does not diminish my contribution to my world.

46) Although it appears like it was a poor decision to accept a direct care employment at a psychiatric hospital as I reflect of my nine years of experience, it became apparent that I have learnt and experienced enough for my next assignment.

47) Self-encouragement and determination is a resolve of the heart.

48) If you are determined to make a difference, and do the things that make a difference you will eventually make a difference.

49) Good things do not come easy

50) Short cuts will cut your life short.

51) Those who look ahead move ahead.

52) Life is all about making an impact. In your life time strive to make an impact in your community.

53) Make friends and connect with people who are moving ahead of you in life.

54) If you can look around well you have come a long way in your life, made a lot of difference and realized a lot of success in life.

55) If you are my old friend, hurry up to reach out to me before I become a stranger to you.

56) Everything I am blessed with inspirations from God, that change my definition and interpretation of the world around me.

57) I thought I was stagnant and lonely until I looked around and noticed my children running around and my wife cooking.

58) At 40 I resigned my Job to seek the Lord forever.

59) My ministry took a drastic rise to the top when the wisdom of God visited me with knowledge and understanding.

60) You will be a better person if you understand the characteristics of your personality – your mood swings attitudes and habits.

61) It is the seed of love you sow into the heart of a child and a woman that you reap in due time.

62) Love is not selfish, love share everything including the concealed secrets of the mind.

63) As long as you have a prayer life and a bible; you will never feel lonely, rejected and idle in the race of life.

64) When good friends disconnect from you, let them go, they might have seen something new in a different direction.

65) Confidence in yourself and in God is the only way to bring you out of captivity

66) Never train a child to waste his/her time.

67) The mind is the greatest assets of a great future.

68) You walk by common sense run by principles and fly by instruction.

69) Those who fly in flight of life fly alone.

70) Up in the air you are alone. No one can toll you accept the compass of knowledge and information

71) I have seen a tolling vehicle I have seen a tolling ship I have never seen a tolling airplane.

72) I exercise my judgment and make a decision every minute of the day.

73) Decisions are crucial, critical and vital with reference to your future.

74) So many people wish for a great future. You can only work towards a great future.

75) Your celebrity status began when you discovered your talent. What are you good at? Work at it with all commitment.

76) Prayers will sustain you but the wisdom of God will prosper you.

77) When I met Oyedepo, his teachings changed my perspective, but when I met Ibiyeomie; His teaching changed my perception.

78) I will be successful in ministry if only I concentrate and focus my energy in the work of the ministry.

79) It took the late Dr. Vincent Pearle Norman's book to open my mind towards kingdom success.

CHAPTER 4

PRAYER OF SALVATION

And it shall come to pass, that whosoever shall call on the name of the Lord shall be delivered: for in mount Zion and in Jerusalem shall be deliverance, as the Lord hath said, and in the remnant whom the Lord shall call. (Joel 2:32)

Salvation means deliverance of our soul from destruction and from sin and its punishment. Jesus Christ is the flat form for salvation. There is no other name under which we all can be saved. *"Neither is there salvation in any other: for there is none other name under heaven given among men, whereby we must be saved."* (Acts 4:12)

A correction officer in charge of a jail house who witnessed Apostle Paul and Silas angelic break out was surprised of that miracle and he said…..

"And brought them out, and said, Sirs, what must I do to be saved? And they said, Believe on the Lord Jesus Christ, and thou shalt be saved, and thy house."
Acts 16:30-31

----We must embrace Salvation, otherwise we are heading into hell----

"For with the heart man believeth unto righteousness; and with the mouth confession is made unto salvation."
Romans 10:10

To qualify for salvation, we must be born again!

The word says as many as received him, to them gave He power to become the sons of God. Even to them that believe on his name.

To qualify for divine visitation do the following sincerely

1) Acknowledge that you are a sinner and that He died for you. Rom 3:23.

2) Repent of your sins. Acts 3:19, Luke 13:5, 2Peter 3:9

3) Believe in your heart that Jesus died for your sin. Romans 10:10

4) Confess Jesus as the Lord over your life. Romans 10:10, Acts 2:21

Now repeat this Prayer after me

Say Lord Jesus, I accept you today, as my Lord and my savior, forgive me of my sins wash me with your blood. Right now, I believe, I am sanctified, I am save, I am free, I am free from the Power of sin to serve the Lord Jesus. Thank you Lord for saving me. Amen.

Congratulations: YOU ARE NOW...

...A BORN AGAIN CHRISTIAN AGAIN I SAY TO YOU - CONGRATULATIONS!

MIRACLE CARE OUTREACH

"...But that the members should have the same care one for another"
1 Cor 12:25

We are all members of the body of Christ. Jesus commanded us to love our neighbor as ourselves. This includes caring for one another as a member of one body. True love is expressed in caring and giving. The word says for God so Love He gave….

Reach out to someone in need of Jesus, help someone in crisis find Christ. Look out and prove your love to Jesus by caring and inviting your friends and associates to find Jesus the Healer.

Invite your friends to our Home Care Cell Fellowship (Miracle chapel Intl Satellite fellowship) In the USA at 33 Schley Street Newark New Jersey 07112.

If you are in Nigeria—MIRACLE OF GOD MINISTRIES, A.K.A "MIRACLE CHAPEL INTL" Mpama –Egbu-Owerri Imo state Nigeria.

(Home Care Cell fellowship Group). We meet every Tuesday at 6:00pm-7:00pm.

LIFE IS NOT ALL ABOUT DURATION BUT ITS ALL ABOUT DONATION

What does the above statement mean?....

Life consists not in accumulation of material wealth.(Luke12:15) But it's all about liberality.... meaning- what you can give and share with others. (Proverb 11:25) When you live for others--You live forever- because you out live your generation by the legacy you live behind after you depart into glory to be with the Lord. But when you live to yourself - you are reduced to self—you are easily forgotten when you die and depart in glory.

Permit me to admonish you today to live your life to be a blessing to a soul connected to you today. I want you to know that so many souls are connected and looking up to you, and through you so many souls will be saved and rescued from destruction. Will you disciple someone today to find Jesus Christ?

As a genuine Christian; it is your duty to evangelize Jesus Christ to all you meet on your way. Jesus is still in the healing business-Jesus is still doing miracles from time of old to now. Therefore tell someone about Jesus Christ today, disciple and bring them to Church. *Philip findeth Nathanael...* (John 1:45)

Please to prove the sincerity of your love for God today; please become a soul winner. The dignity of your Christianity is hidden in your boldness to proclaim and evangelize Jesus Christ to all you meet on your way. There is a question mark on the integrity of your Christianity until you become a life soul winner. Invite someone to join us worship the Lord Jesus this coming Sunday. Amen.

MIRACLE OF GOD MINISTRIES

PILLARS OF THE COMMISSION

We Believe Preach and Practice the following

1) We believe and preach Salvation to every living human being

2) We believe and preach Repentance and forgiveness of sins

3) We believe and preach the baptism of the Holy Spirit and Spiritual gifts

4) We believe and teach the Prosperity

5) We believe and preach Divine Healing and Miracles (Signs &Wonder)

6) We believe and preach Faith

7) We believe and Proclaim the Power of God (Supernatural)

8) We believe and Proclaim Praise & Worship to God

9) We believe and preach Wisdom

10) We believe and preach Holiness (Consecration)

11) We believe and preach Vision

12) We believe and teach the Word of God

13) We believe and teach Success

14) We believe and practice Prayer

15) We believe and teach Deliverance

This 15 stones form the Pillars of Our Commission. Become part of this church family and follow this great move of God.

----MY HEART FELT PRAYER FOR YOU----

It is always my joy and pleasure to see you saved. It is always my joy to know that you will make heaven with us. But I rejoice more with you, when I hear your testimonies and encounters with God. One of the reason why I write is to spread the gospel of Jesus Christ in print. I therefore encourage you to get in touch with any of our materials. We offer so many materials available for you, from books, magazine, mp3 tapes, sermon outlines, and brochure. I guarantee you, it will highly help your faith and your walk with our Lord Jesus Christ.

Now let me Pray for you:

Father God I thank you because all things work together for our good. Lord even today demonstrate your awesome power that is unique and unlimited in dimension unto this precious loved one reading this book now. Lord God increase their faith by granting them unprecedented testimonies. Lord do that no man can do and take all the glory.
In Jesus Mighty name. Amen

BEWARE LEST WE FORGET THE LORD

" Then beware lest thou forget the Lord, which brought thee forth out of the land of Egypt, from the house of bondage."
Deut 6:12

In my own opinion knowing God is a personal experience. We are instructed to *"...work out your own salvation with fear and trembling. For it is God which worketh in you both to will and to do of his good pleasure."* (Phil 2:12-13)

It has always been my vision to see you experience an encounter with our Lord Jesus Christ. A lot of church folks have indirectly denied him, but I tell you the truth as long as you embrace him invisibly , He will do great things in your life.

We must always practice the ritual of daily devotion and prayer as a lifestyle. You can join our prayer-line 712-432-0360-code 478238 every Mondays, Wednesday, and Saturdays eastern time. More also you can come worship with us together at our worship center 343 Sanford avenue Newark New Jersey 07106.

- Do not forget God is spirit, therefore we must worship him in spirit and in truth. God is not a man that he should lie, nor the son of man that he should repent.

- Learn to honor the presence of God in your life.

- Embrace the acts and hand of God in your life.

- Respect and reverence God in your life time.

- Help spread the gospel of Jesus by winning soul for the Kingdom of God.

- Finally I must talk to you about eternity! Heaven is real and we all must make conscious plan to make it at last. I hate to tell you more about hell but we must repent of our sins forsake our sins confess Jesus as Lord and embrace the gift of Salvation for us to make heaven. We must live a righteous life, worthy of emulation for others to copy for the Kingdom of God.

WE MUST TURN TO GOD

"It is written For God so loved the world, that he gave his only begotten Son, that whosoever believeth in him should not perish, but have everlasting life."
John 3:16

We must be determine to seek the Lord forever. Heaven is a race that is judge on individual merits. It is written " For every man shall bear his own burden." This heavenly race that we are preaching is for the salvation of our soul. We all must genuinely repent and seek the Lord for ever more. I encourage you not to let the news media the television to deceive us.

---- *Be conscious of eternity*----

Eternity is real and heaven is real!!
We must turn to God for the salvation of our life.

"If I shut up heaven that there be no rain, or if I command the locusts to devour the land, or if I send pestilence among my people; If my people, which are called by my name, shall humble themselves, and pray, and seek my face, and turn from their wicked ways; then will I hear from heaven, and will forgive their sin, and will heal their land."
2 Chronicle 7:13-14.

"For all have sinned, and come short of the glory of God;"
Romans 3:23

"For the wages of sin is death; but the gift of God is eternal life through Jesus Christ our Lord."
Romans 6:23

I encourage and admonish you to go all out for God. Watch and see the rewards and turn over that will envelope your life.

ABOUT THE AUTHOR

Rev Franklin N Abazie is the founding and Presiding Pastor of Miracle of God Ministries with headquarters in Newark, New Jersey USA and a branch church in Owerri- Imo State Nigeria. He is following the footsteps of one of his mentors, Oral Roberts (Healing Evangelist) of the blessed memory. The Lord passed Oral Roberts healing mantle two days before he went to be with the Lord at age 91 into the hand of healing evangelist-Rev Franklin N Abazie in a vision.

In all his services the Power and Presence of God is present to heal all in his audience. He is an ordained man of God with a Healing Ministry reviving the healing and miracle ministry of Jesus Christ of Nazareth.

Pastor Franklin N Abazie, is called by God with a unique mandate: **"THE MOMENT IS DUE TO IMPACT YOUR WORLD THROUGH THE REVIVAL OF THE HEALING & MIRACLE MINISTRY OF JESUS CHRIST OF NAZARETH**

I AM SENDING YOU TO RESTORE HEALTH UNTO THEE AND I WILL HEAL THEE OF THY WOUNDS. SAID THE LORD OF HOST"

He is a gifted ardent Teacher of the word of God who operates also in the office of a Prophet, generating and attracting undeniable signs & wonders, special miracles and healings, with apostolic fireworks of the Holy Ghost. He is the founding and presiding senior Pastor of this fast growing Healing ministry. He has written over 86 inspirational, healing and transforming books covering almost all aspect of divine healing and life. He is happily married and blessed with children.

BOOKS BY REV FRANKLIN N ABAZIE

1) The Outcome of Faith
2) Understanding the secret of prevailing Prayers
3) Commanding Abundance
4) Understanding the secret of the man God uses
5) Activating my due Season
6) Overcoming Divine Verdicts
7) The Outcome of Divine Wisdom
8) Understanding God's Restoration Mandate
9) Walking in the Victory and Authority of the truth
10) Gods Covenant Exemption
11) Destiny Restoration Pillars
12) Provoking Acceptable Praise
13) Understanding Divine Judgment
14) Activating Angelic Re-enforcement
15) Provoking Un-Merited Favor
16) The Benefits of the Speaking faith
17) Understanding Divine Arrangement
18) How to Keep Your Healing
19) Understanding the mysteries of the Speaking Faith
20) Understanding the mysteries of Prophetic healing
21) Operating under the Rules of Creative Healing
22) Understanding the joy of Breakthrough
23) Understanding the Mystery of Breakthrough
24) Understanding Divine Prosperity
25) Understanding Divine Healing
26) Retaining Your Inheritance
27) Overcoming confusing Spirit
28) Commanding Angelic Escorts
29) Enforcing Your inheritance in Christ Jesus

30) Understanding Your Guardian Angels
31) Overcoming the Dominion of Sin
32) Understanding the Voice of God
33) The Outstanding benefits of the Anointing
34) The Audacity of the Blood of Jesus
35) Walking in the Reality of the Anointing
36) Escaping the Nightmare of Poverty
37) Understanding Your Harvest Season
38) Activating Your Success Buttons
39) Overcoming the forces of Darkness
40) Overcoming the devices of the devil
41) Overcoming Demonic agents
42) Overcoming the sorrows of failure
43) Rejecting the Sorrows of failure
44) Resisting the Sorrows of Poverty
45) The Restoring broken Marriages.
46) Redeeming Your Days
47) The force of Vision
48) Overcoming the forces of ignorance
49) Understanding the sacrifice of small beginning
50) The might of small beginning
51) Understanding the mysteries of Prophesy
52) Overcoming Dream nightmares
53) Breaking the shackles of the curse of the law
54) Understanding the Joy of harvest
55) Wisdom for Signs & Wonders
56) Wisdom for generational Impact
57) Wisdom for Marriage Stability
58) Understanding the number of your Days
59) Enforcing Your Kingdom Rights
60) Escaping the traps of immoralities
61) Escaping the trap of Poverty
62) Accessing Biblical Prosperity

63) Accessing True Riches in Christ
64) Silencing the Voice of the Accuser
65) Overcoming the forces of oppositions
66) Quenching the voice of the avenger
67) Silencing demonic Prediction & Projection
68) Silencing Your Mocker
69) Understanding the Power of the Holy Ghost
70) Understanding the baptism of Power
71) The Mystery of the Blood of Jesus
72) Understanding the Mystery of Sanctification
73) Understanding the Power of Holiness
74) Understanding the forces of Purity & Righteousness
75) Activating the Forces of Vengeance
76) Appreciating the Mystery of Restoration
77) Overcoming the Projection & Prediction of the enemy
78) Engaging the mystery of the blood
79) Commanding the Power of the Speaking faith
80) Uprooting the forces against Your Rising
81) Overcoming mere success syndrome
82) Understanding Divine Sentence
83) Understanding the Mystery of Praise
84) Understanding the Author of Faith
85) The Mystery of the finisher of faith
86) Attracting Supernatural Favor

MIRACLE OF GOD MINISTRIES

*NIGERIA CRUSADE
2012*

MIRACLE OF GOD MINISTRIES

NIGERIA CRUSADE 2012

MIRACLE OF GOD MINISTRIES

NIGERIA CRUSADE 2012

www.ingramcontent.com/pod-product-compliance
Lightning Source LLC
Chambersburg PA
CBHW070055120526
44588CB00033B/1536